Vivacious Biography with Lessons to Learn from E.A.R.L. DMX for Life with Bonus Sections

By JJ Vance

Table of Contents

Disclaimer and Note to Readers:

This is an unofficial tribute book to DMX from a fan, for a fan to support his legacy.

The information in this book has been provided for educational and entertainment purposes only.

The information contained in this book has been compiled from sources deemed reliable and it is accurate to the best of the Author's knowledge; however, the Author cannot guarantee its accuracy and validity and cannot be held liable for any errors or omissions.

The fact that an individual or organization is referred to in this document as a citation or source of information does not imply that the author or publisher endorses the information that the individual or organization provided. This is an unofficial fan tribute book and has not been approved or endorsed by the DMX or his associates.

Before You Go Any Further, Download Your Free Gift!

Thanks for checking out **"Vivacious Biography with Lessons to Learn from E.A.R.L. DMX for Life with Bonus Sections"** – You have made a wise choice in picking up this book!

Because you're about to discover many interesting tidbits of DMX you've never knew before!

But before you go any further, I'd like to offer you a free gift.

My Ultimate Collection of Links to DMX's YouTube Videos!

If you're a DMX fan, you'll DROOL over this!

But I'll take it down if too many people claim it as it's my personal treasure. *Don't miss out!*

Get it before it expires here:
http://bit.ly/DMXBonus

Or Scan the QR Code:

DMX: INTRODUCTION

If there was ever a genre of music that many thought would die out quickly, it was Rap.

Years ago, when rap began to go mainstream, there was no shortage of people who were dead set against the success of the rap genre. Fortunately, the fan base of rap music continued to rapidly grow as artists continued to release their art even though they were facing immense opposition. Everyone from parents to politicians seemed determined to suppress this art form. But rap proved to them that it was there to stay.

Decades later, rap is one of the most popular genres in the world right now. Rap music and the lovers of this art form around the globe owe quite a lot of this genre's success to artists who continued to release great music, pushing this genre forward.

From Grandmaster Flash to Notorious B.I.G and Tupac, who were there at the very start of mainstream hip-hop, to one person who contributed immensely to this generation of rap – DMX.

Earl Simmons, more popularly known by his stage name DMX, short for "Dark Man X," was an American rapper, songwriter, and actor. His role in advancing rap music can't be challenged.

DMX was known and loved for his raw, authentic music, which resonated with his audience, as well as his down-to-earth nature. He stayed true to his roots in the streets even after he had built a successful career and a comfortable life for himself.

He was a great songwriter and an amazing rapper. In addition to all this, he was real and open in his music. DMX was a unique rapper in that he never gave in to the pretence that had become commonplace among the rich and famous hip-hop artists of the time. All this made it that much easier for his art to connect with his

listeners. It comes as no surprise then that X was able to sell more

than 74 million records globally.

But it wasn't always this rosy for DMX, who had been rapping

for about 10 years before the release, *It's Dark and Hell is Hot,* his

debut album in 1998.

Growing up was filled with struggles of all kinds for the young

DMX, then only known as Earl. He had an abusive mother, a largely

absent father, lived in the projects in abject poverty, and slept on the

floor with roaches and rodents as his bedtime companions. His

mother's several, constantly changing boyfriends were also

physically abusive and played no small part in making his childhood

hellish.

Earl Simmons was a very intelligent child. Early IQ tests showed that he had a higher intelligence level than most kids, two or three grades above him. But this didn't make school any easy for him. Young DMX was known for his misbehavior. He would act out in school and even got violent towards his schoolmates and his teachers.

On his report cards, he was described as a bright kid who was manipulative. And on at least one occasion, young DM was expelled from school because of his bad behavior.

As it turns out, it wasn't only Earl's school that didn't want him around. On multiple occasions, his mother sent him to live at group homes. Once when he was just 10 years old, after he had just been expelled from school, his mom deceived him into thinking they were going to check out a group home named Children's Village. Once they got there, she checked him into the home. Young DMX hadn't even gotten the chance to bring his clothes from home.

This betrayal from his mother ended up being one of the most prominent defining moments of X's life. According to the rapper, the experience taught him to hide away and bury the things that bothered him.

His 18-month-long stay in this group home was an eventful one. He and another child in the home were arrested for arson. They both had attempted to set the school on fire. Not long after that, Earl nearly killed his co-conspirator. This led to him being sent into solitary confinement. This stint in solitary would be just the first of many more bouts DMX would be sentenced to in his lifetime.

After returning home from his stay at the group home, Earl began to attempt to escape his mother's abusiveness.

At the age of 14, Earl took to the streets. He began sleeping on the streets of Yonkers, New York. He would sleep in Salvation

Army clothing bins and attempt to make friends with stray dogs that he found on the street. During this time, his love for dogs, which he portrays in some of his songs, began to develop.

When his mother found out about his habit of wandering the streets, she enrolled him into another boys' group home. It was in this home that DMX discovered his love for hip-hop. He became an incredibly skilled beatboxer and even adopted the name 'DMX' from the Oberheim DMX digital drum machine, an instrument he played while at the boys' home. Later on in his career, the name "DMX" was interpreted as "Dark Man X."

When he returned home from the boys' group home, Earl Simmons got acquainted with a locally respected rapper named Ready Ron, who was impressed with the 14-year-old's beatboxing skills. Ready Ron asked Earl to partner up with him, encouraging the young artist to take his music seriously and offering him some much-needed mentorship. Earl adopted DMX as his official rap name and worked with Ready Ron for a while.

As a freshman in high school, Earl was hardly interested in academics. He had bad grades and rarely ever attended classes. His interest lay in two places; the track team and robbing people.

With an absent father and a struggling mother, Earl didn't have enough money for anything – not clothes, track equipment, or food. This pushed the young teenager into a life of crime. He began robbing people on the street, in school, outside supermarkets, etc.

His criminal activities evolved from petty robberies to more advanced crimes like car theft and even some home break-ins, which the rapper admitted he was never a fan of.

Earl Simmons got away with some of these crimes. But at other times, he wasn't as lucky, which resulted in constant trips in and out of jail.

DMX got his first bout of solitary confinement in an actual jail after being pulled over by the cops during a joy ride, he and a friend took in a stolen car. For a week, he was stuck in a small, 6 x 9 cell. But this wasn't as bad as he may have thought or as his sadistic jailers may have hoped. The budding rapper turned his stint in solitary confinement into a meaningful time which led to an artistic breakthrough.

According to the rapper, he wrote pages upon pages of rhymes – more than he had ever written before. He experimented with his style, flows, and different techniques. By the time his period of solitary confinement was over, DMX had emerged as a much better rapper than he was when he had gone in.

In and out of jail, Earl's life was characterized by rap battles and robbery. He would walk the streets of New York with his huge bulldog named Boomer, looking for a victim to rob, and sometimes, he would come across a rap battle, which to the young rapper, was just as good.

DMX began producing his own mixtapes where he would rap to instrumentals from other songs. He sold these records on the streets and street corners of New York. Soon, his work began to pay off, and he began to build a local fan base for himself all over New York.

This was the beginning of his big break as a rapper.

In 1991, a magazine publication named *The Source* featured DMX in its *Unsigned Hype* column. This column featured hip-hop artists that weren't signed to a record label.

This column put DMX on a pedestal and played a significant role in bringing him into the public's eye. In 1992, one year after the column about DMX was written, Columbia Records signed him to their subsidiary label Ruffhouse Records. That same year, DMX dropped his debut single, "Born Loser."

The bars in this piece were close to home, as is typical of DMX's music. He talks about how hard the ghetto was and how he had to steal to survive. DMX rapped about eating turkey-flavored Now & Laters for Thanksgiving and other struggles he had to face as part of his everyday life.

Unfortunately for DMX, this single flopped. It got very little serious attention, and Columbia Records decided to drop him and focus their attention and resources on two of their platinum artists.

This wasn't the end for DMX, whose reputation had caught the attention of Joaquin "Waah" Dean, a Harlem native who wanted to get off the streets for good and enter into the music industry as the co-founder of his own record label, Ruff Ryders Entertainment.

According to Waah, record labels like Columbia had no idea what to do with an artist like DMX. With DMX and some other new artists on board, Ruff Ryders Entertainment was ready to launch. All they needed was some backing.

With the help of some well-placed connections, they were able to get an executive from Def Jam Records to watch their artists battle each other in the studio during a Ruff Ryders studio session. This executive liked what he saw, and Ruff Ryders got their deal with Def Jam Recordings.

Ruff Ryders had the backing they needed and the truckload of talent that was DMX. Next, they needed to get the attention of the public. They had to drop a track that would create a buzz and get people talking about DMX and the Def Jam deal.

Early in 1998, his first major-label single, *Get at Me Dog,* dropped. The waves this single created were unlike anything at that time. It dominated the radio waves and the minds of almost every fan of rap music at that time.

But even before then, he had already become the hottest new rapper on the scene because of his cameos on The Lox's "Money, Power, and Respect," LL Cool J's "4,3,2,1...," and Mase's "24 Hours to Live."

In May 1998, he released *It's Dark and Hell is Hot,* his first major-label album. This album debuted at number one and sold over

5 million copies. December that same year, he dropped *Flesh of My Flesh, Blood of My Blood,* his second album. And again, this album also debuted at number one on the Billboard 200 chart in the United States.

DMX dropping two albums in one year is a decision that was fueled by Lyor Cohen, the Def Jam executive. As the story goes, Lyor promised DMX a million dollars if he could pull it off. Two albums in one calendar year must have been a tough feat even for a rap god like DMX. But if anyone could over-deliver, that was precisely what DMX did. His second album got a triple platinum. DMX simultaneously managed to release a legendary album, just six months after his debut album, while keeping his vow that the album would be his "connection to the community." Just as he had promised, he could say what was on the minds of his people and make "one brotha's pain understood by the world."

It wasn't long into his career as a rapper had fully taken off before DMX began being featured in movies and TV shows.

DMX's career was typified by hit songs, viral albums, major award nominations, and wins – all punctuated once in a while by brief stints in jail.

Unfortunately, DMX also struggled with drugs. Hollywood and its attendant "yes men" didn't help matters. Gradually, his drug use began to consume him. He got in trouble with the law for everything from animal cruelty, to tax evasion, to drug possession and much more.

However, things seemed to be looking up for the legendary rapper when he got out of jail early in 2019. The rapper re-signed with Def Jam and gave a powerful performance at a Kanye West Sunday Service.

Unfortunately, on the 4th of March 2021, DMX's journey

ended when a heart attack landed him in the hospital, bringing his

career, and eventually his life, to an end.

Earl Simmons died as the first rapper to have two albums go

platinum in the same year and the first one to have his first five

studio albums debut at #1.

DMX's music touched countless lives. Though he was far from

perfect – with over 30 different bouts of jail time – he used his music

as a tool to affect the lives he came in contact with and millions more

that he would never meet.

EARLY LIFE

When DMX was born, he wasn't DMX. As all great stories begin, the great rap legend was nothing more than an innocent baby. His mother named him Earl Simmons.

Earl Simmons was born on the 18th of December 1970 – which, in what is probably one of the biggest coincidences of DMX's life, was the year of the dog. He was born in Mount Vernon, New York. And although his career had him traveling different places around the world and the country, it was clear throughout his life that New York was more than his birthplace; it was his home.

Earl Simmons was born disadvantaged from the very start. His family was dysfunctional – with an abusive mother and an absentee father – and broke. They lived in poor conditions and depended on food stamps to get through.

What's more, Earl Simmons was born with not-so-good health. He had a couple of allergies that he inherited from his mother and bronchial asthma, which he got from his father. His early life was filled with several trips to the hospital's emergency room. Sometimes, he would have to spend the entire night there. And other times, he would spend days in the hospital.

On different occasions, young Earl would wake up in the middle of the night, unable to breathe. Apart from the intense treatments, he was given while at the hospital, he also had prescriptions for drugs he could take at home. Sometimes, instead of improving his condition, these drugs would make him sicker.

Earl's mother, Arnett Simmons, was just 19 years old when she gave birth to him. But even at such a young age, Earl wasn't Arnett's first child; he was the second. At the time of her son's birth, Arnett already had a two-year-old daughter named Bonita.

Earl and his sister Bonita had different fathers. His father's

name was Joe Barker.

Joe Barker and Arnett Simmons met in high school about one

or two years before Earl was born. The two teenagers – Arnett and

Joe – were a cute couple. But that was about it.

Joe Barker was the kind of guy that the ladies loved. He knew

how to get their attention and so always had a lot of girlfriends.

Similarly, Arnett Barker was a catch herself. She was pretty, and guys

found her very attractive. Arnett was the kind of woman that turned

heads as she walked down the street.

On the surface, the two were a picture-perfect couple. The

handsome, charming young man and the beautiful, attractive young

lady. They seemed to be perfect for each other.

Yet, despite the appearances, Earl Simmons' father and mother were never really close. Yes, they were in a relationship, but that relationship never really was anything more than sex.

It must have come as little of a surprise when Joe Barker, who was only 18 years old himself when his son was born, didn't want Arnett to have their child.

After Earl's birth, Joe Barker was seldom around. By that time, what little chemistry existed between the two teenagers was long gone.

Joe never considered living with his baby's mother and child, and he didn't help raise the baby. However, he did show up once in a while. Joe would randomly and spontaneously make an appearance at their home. Occasionally, he would take Earl with him to sell paintings that he'd made himself.

Joe Barker was a watercolor artist who was obsessed with art. Painting was his passion, and he dedicated most of his time to it, not even bothering to get another job. Barker would paint watercolors of street scenes in New York and sell his works at local fairs and malls. Almost entirely consumed by his love for painting, Joe would choose to go homeless when his paintings weren't bringing in money rather than get a paying job.

The few occasions Earl spent time with his father were enough to get him interested in drawing. At a young age, Earl's artistic talent began to become evident. At six years old, his room was covered with pictures he had drawn himself, and as he grew older, he got better and better and began to do more with his skills. He would make sketches of his sister at her request and even carve drawings into wood.

Unfortunately, when DMX was in elementary school, his father upped and left New York for good. He moved to Philadelphia because he thought it would be a better place to earn a living by

selling his paintings. And just like that, he went out of Earl's life

completely.

Growing up with his mother as his only stable guardian was a

terrible experience for young DMX. His mother claimed to be

religious – a Jehovah's Witness to be precise – yet, with the help of

her numerous boyfriends and hookups, she managed to make Earl's

life hell.

Early on, Earl didn't mind the Jehovah's Witness part of his

upbringing. He enjoyed most of it. He liked the services the Jehovah's

Witnesses held at the local Kingdom Hall, traveling to conferences.

He liked the books of Bible stories and The Watchtower magazine

that they gave out.

However, his fondness for religion was soon taken away after an accident that almost took his life.

While he was still a young child, Earl had many close encounters with death. Most of the time, these almost fatal events occurred because of his terrible asthma. Once, he had an asthma attack that was so bad that, according to his sister Bonita, Earl's heart stopped beating.

But his brushes with death weren't always caused by his medical condition. One time, he was playing on the street by himself when he saw a dime. Excited by the money he found, young Earl managed to summon enough courage to cross the street to his prize, which was a considerable feat for a child as young as he was at the time.

On his way back across the street, he got hit by a car.

Fortunately for him, he didn't break any bones, and none of his

injuries were too severe, so he was better within a few weeks.

As it turns out, the man who had hit him had not only beaten

a red light but was also driving drunk. About a month after the

accident took place, a man from the insurance company came over

to his house to offer his mother a settlement which, according to

Earl, was worth ten thousand dollars.

Earl believed that if his mother held out a bit, she could get

the insurance company to pay even more than ten thousand dollars.

But instead, his mother made a decision that frustrated Earl

so much, he would never forget it. She turned the money down. Her

reason? Her Jehovah's Witness beliefs required her to be self-

sufficient. Considering that she was living off public assistance during the first few years of Earl's life and that the Jehovah's Witness

doctrine at the time didn't prohibit members from receiving

settlements or even suing, her decision was nothing short of odd.

After that event, Earl wasn't nearly as fond of the Jehovah's

Witness religion as he used to be.

When Arnett Simmons found out she was pregnant with Earl,

it wasn't good news to her. Her daughter, Bonita, was just two years

old, and she hadn't planned on having another child. At least not at

that time.

Arnett's sister Laverne took Bonita off her hands while she

moved into a home for unwed mothers in Mount Vernon. One year

after Earl was born and Bonita was back, Arnett's mother died.

Arnett had to find a place of her own, so she moved out of Mount

Vernon to Yonkers, where she had a higher chance of finding a place

she could afford.

For a while, the family lived in a small, one-bedroom

apartment, but that didn't stop his mother from having men over.

She had numerous boyfriends at different times, and she had even

named her son after one of them – Earl Scott.

Arnett was trying to build a better life for herself and to get

off of public assistance. Even when she moved herself and her kid

into a nicer place in a set of projects called School Street, the living

conditions didn't get much better. Especially not for Earl. In their

new location, Earl had a room of his own but still had to sleep on the

living room floor most of the time because of his uncle Robert.

Robert, who was more fondly known by Arnett's kids as Uncle

Pinky, was Arnett's younger brother who worked as a handyman. He was always bringing ladies over, and because none of them agreed to sleep on the couch, Earl had to give up his bedroom most of the time and sleep on the living room floor instead.

At first, he didn't mind this setup much because it gave him the chance to sneak some food from the refrigerator while everyone else was asleep. And most of the time, he'd find a way to blame someone else in the house.

But as a few days turned into weeks and months and Uncle Pinky was still around, sleeping on the floor got frustrating for Earl. The young boy had to deal with roaches and rodents, which made it understandably difficult for him to get a good night's rest. He would get bitten by bugs and tormented by noisy rodents.

To make living in the School Street projects even worse for Earl, his mother never let them leave the apartment unless they were going to school or running an errand. Plus, Earl's mother seemed to always find a reason to beat him.

31

When it came to giving her son a good beating, Arnett never ran out of ways to do that. She would use anything – from her hands to the stick of a broom. And if she got tired or just wasn't in the mood, one of her boyfriends – or even the mailman (whom she also hooked up with) – could take over from her and give young DMX a whopping.

Nothing, it seemed, was off-limits for Arnett and her boyfriends to use as a cane – hangers, extension cords, belts, you name it. Sometimes, she would even insult him verbally, telling young DMX that he wasn't shit, "just like his father."

But the beatings didn't seem to make things any better. Earl's behavior only seemed to get worse and worse. Both at home and in school.

While in school, Earl was quite an intelligent student. An IQ test he was given showed that his intelligence was higher than kids two or three years older than him. His teachers described him as a bright student. But it wasn't long before they began to notice that he was not only bright but manipulative too.

Earl was a kid that was difficult to understand. To his teachers, his excellent academic performance seemed to stand in stark contrast to his delinquent behaviors. They didn't know how to handle him.

Once, his school insisted on making him repeat an entire school year because of his behavior. He was saved by his mother, who insisted that his grades were too good for them to do that. After all, he was top of his class at the time.

In elementary school, Earl was taking advanced classes and winning spelling competitions regularly. But he was also getting bored, and in an attempt to keep his mind occupied, Earl would get into one mischief or the other.

Earl went from shooting spitballs and throwing erasers at other pupils to throwing chairs at teachers. Once, he even stabbed a classmate with a pencil.

On several occasions, he got detention as punishment for his misdeeds. Still, even this wasn't enough to get him to stop. On the contrary, Earl enjoyed and looked forward to detentions. He got to stay behind after school and after all the other kids had left. This allowed him to steal toys from their desks once there was no teacher

in the detention classroom.

At home, his mother also didn't seem to know what to do

with him. She kept him indoors, not letting him play with his friends

or other kids in the neighborhood. When he stayed out late without

informing his mother on at least two occasions, it didn't end up well

for him either time.

One summer, his mother locked him up in his room, not

allowing him to come out at all except to use the bathroom.

Still, the beatings continued. One night, Earl got up from bed

to drink some water when he saw his mother's notebook lying open

on the kitchen table. He looked into it and saw something that in his

mind was wrong. So, he got an eraser and began to erase it, thinking

he was helping. When his mother caught him doing this, she got so mad that she picked up a broom to give him a beating. And while

giving the young boy a whopping, she beat two teeth out of his

mouth with the broom.

Once, the main office of his school began to notice that he

showed up at school bruised or injured on several occasions in one

way or the other. When they discovered it was his mother giving him

the injuries, the court got involved.

Arnett insisted that Earl's bad behavior forced her to treat

him the way she did. So, the court suggested that she take Earl to a

child psychologist.

On their first meeting, Earl grew to distrust the psychologist.

He didn't talk to him about anything, and at the end of all the

sessions he attended, nothing had changed.

If anything had changed at all, Earl had gotten worse. He had completely lost control and was causing chaos at school.

The court had to step in since it seemed his mother couldn't keep him out of trouble. And that was how he was sent to a group home – his first group home.

He was ten years old at the time, and the institution's name was Julia Dyckman Andrus Children's Home. His school had expelled him, and his "sentence" was set at 18 months long at the group home. A ten-year-old Earl would be away from home, and his family was, in all likelihood, hoping something miraculous would happen and Earl would come out rehabilitated. Unfortunately, that wasn't the case. Far from it, in fact.

Earl enjoyed his time at the group home; at least he did at first. He ate 3 meals a day with dessert and was given a snack at night. The rooms had televisions, and the students got paid for the chores that they did. The school provided them with extra money to buy gifts for their families at Christmas time, and in the spring, they were taken on vacation.

Everything was going fine until Earl got into big trouble. He and another kid had almost burnt an entire building down. According to DMX, all they wanted to do was find out if the building floor would turn blue like the flames.

The school acknowledged that the incident was an accident, but Earl got arrested for arson because the janitor had heard him say, "where's the match?" But his co-conspirator, a kid named Adam, wasn't charged because, unlike in Earl's case where the janitor heard him ask for a match, there wasn't any evidence against Adam.

This wasn't the first time that young DMX had been sent to jail. When he was just seven years old, he got caught shoplifting a box of pies from a supermarket.

Even though he was just ten years old, going to jail was not a new experience for Earl. But this time was different for him, and he was particularly unhappy, not just because he was being punished, but because his co-conspirator was getting off scot-free.

Earl began to hate him, and the two began to fight daily. Earl felt like killing Adam, literally. Then one day, he tried to do just that. He went up to Adam and squeezed his neck in a chokehold until the kid's face turned blue, and he fell unconscious.

Adam's parents didn't hesitate to press charges.

It was at this point that Earl made it clear that they were going to need more than a group home to rehabilitate him. His elementary school had put him out, and now Julia Dyckman Andrus Children's Home was about to do the same.

He was removed from the normal school population and put into isolation. Young DMX did his schoolwork away from the other kids and ate his meals by himself. This would be his first taste of solitary confinement, but it definitely wouldn't be his last.

When he got back from Andrus Children's Home after 18 months, Earl wasn't rehabilitated. If anything, he had gotten worse. The time spent caged up and isolated away from the other kids drove him to the edge. He stopped caring what others thought and decided to fully embrace all the negative things everyone had said about him — his mother, his teachers, anyone. "Earl is manipulative," they had said. And now, he agreed. He was manipulative, he was a menace, he was a problem. He wasn't going to fight it anymore. Crazy Earl was born.

Back at home, being sent to Andrus Children's Home had given Earl a rep with the neighborhood kids. Only the really bad children get sent to group homes. Earl gladly lived up to the reputation. He took his pranks a step further than anyone else's, and his mischief and recklessness were on a whole other level.

Earl's behavior wasn't the only thing that hadn't improved. It was clear that the situation at home also hadn't changed. But this time, instead of getting a beating, his mother and her boyfriend at the time – the mailman – chose to go another direction in punishing Earl. They grounded him. What started as a weekend locked up in his room turned to a week and then an entire month. For 30 days, Earl wasn't allowed to leave his room except to drink water, eat, and use the bathroom.

But because of the stint, he had spent in isolation while at the children's home, Earl knew how to handle the aloneness well. He created a world for himself, and soon, he learned to shut out everyone else.

The punishment became more of a regular occurrence, and Earl spent most of his time locked up in his room.

After leaving the group home, the decision was made to send Earl to a school on the rich side of the town. It was supposed to be a "progressive" school, but it turned out to be a bad idea. He lasted only two weeks before the school's vice-principal sent him home and decided to send a tutor over to his house instead.

At home, the beatings continued once more. After being sent home that day, he was beaten by his aunt's girlfriend with a wooden club so badly that he was bleeding, and the club started to splinter.

When he got home, his mother said nothing about the bruises and bumps that were all over her son's body. She didn't seem to care. His Uncle Pinky, too, didn't do much about it.

Sometimes, his mother would wake him up at night with spankings. She would sit on him and beat him. On some occasions, she beat him until his asthma started to act up and he wouldn't be able to breathe. And no matter how much he told her that he couldn't breathe, she wouldn't listen. "When I get finished whipping your behind, then I'll take you to the emergency room for your asthma!" she would say. And that's just what she would do.

Things got so bad that young DMX even contemplated killing his mother. He played it through his head several times, but each time, he'd realize that he couldn't go through with it. He hated his mother, yet he loved her.

Through the hard times that he faced at home; Earl had one saving grace – his grandmother. Mary Ella Hollaway was the mother of Joe Baker, Earl's father. Grandma Hollaway had eleven children, but Earl's father was the first to have a child, making Earl her first grandson.

Most of his aunties and uncles were much older than the young DMX, but he had two uncles – Collins (aka Collie or BJ) and Kisley (Buzzy) – who were younger than him. The three of them were like brothers, and Earl, being the eldest, was fond of leading them into mischief.

Earl enjoyed staying at his grandmother's house. He got to eat well, particularly during Sunday dinners which were always a big affair at the Hollaway house. He got to play with his cousins and go outside. He didn't have to live in constant fear of getting beaten. At his grandmother's house, Earl felt loved.

Just like Earl, Grandma Hollaway's grandmother had a bad case of asthma as well. She would watch over him all night whenever he thought he had an asthma attack.

The environment in his grandmother's house was so different from what he lived with when he was with his mother. But unfortunately, his mother and his grandmother didn't like each other.

Grandma Hollaway didn't approve of the way Earl's mother was raising him, and his mother didn't care. "What is your son doing to help?" Arnett would always reply to Grandma Hollaway.

Because of the enmity that existed between the two women, Earl's mother rarely ever let him stay long at his grandmother's place. Most times, he stayed for just a weekend, and that was it.

When things got unbearable at home, Earl would take every opportunity he could to go over to his grandmother's house. But his mother wouldn't let him stay there.

Earl had had enough. He couldn't take any more of the madness that was going on at home. So, he left. He took to the streets.

Earl would leave home for days and only show up randomly back at his mother's house. While on the streets, Earl didn't care that he was out of school or that he didn't have any money. He felt like he was finally in control of his life.

At night, he would spend his time in Salvation Army clothing bins, sleeping amidst all the clothes in there. The bins were the perfect place for him to hide out, especially at night. They were warm, and no one could find him in there.

But there was a problem, living on the streets by himself was lonely. Even all the time he had spent isolated in his room and the children's home wasn't enough to prepare him for the loneliness he would feel on the streets.

Earl needed a companion. And he knew he had found what he was looking for one day when his eyes sighted a dog. The animal was a stray and looked pretty scruffy. Earl tried to approach him, but the dog wasn't having any of it. It ran away.

But young DMX was determined, for three hours, he followed the mutt all over downtown Yonkers. Sometime around noon, the dog finally stopped running away from Earl. Not only did the dog allow Earl to pet him, but he even let him put a makeshift leash around its neck. Later that evening, Earl found some food scraps to feed the dog. He had made a new friend.

From that moment on, Earl's love for dogs began to bloom.

He would adopt stray dogs and take them home to care for them as

his. He had to hide his dogs from his mother because she didn't

approve of them.

He would hide them under his bed and sneak around at night

to bring dogs into the house so that his mother wouldn't see them.

Eventually, he learned to hide them on the roof of their apartment

building. The building had just twelve floors, and his family lived on

the eleventh floor, so all he had to do was walk the dogs up two

flights of stairs to get them to the roof.

Dogs were the only friends Earl had. They were loyal, and as

long as he loved them, they loved him back and would fight to

protect him if they thought he was in danger.

His dog became Earl's weapon of choice when it came to street confrontations in the 'hood. He found out that even people who were bigger and older than him wouldn't mess with him when he was with his dog.

Crazy Earl was running the streets with his loyal canine companions. But what he didn't know was that it was all about to change.

Young DMX was sent to another group home.

Children's Village School for Boys was the name of the group home that would be DMX's residence for over a year. It was 1984, and Earl's mother had made him dress up. They were going for a tour of the group home. At least, that was what Earl's mother made him believe.

When they got to Children's Village School for Boys, they went on a tour of the school, just like his mother had promised. But Earl wasn't expecting it when his mother told him he wasn't going to be following her back home.

She was leaving him in the group home. He had been surprised – after all, he hadn't even gotten to bring an extra pair of clothes. But even more than the shock he felt, Earl felt betrayed by his mother.

With the orange slacks, yellow top, and black shoes on his body, which were the only things he had to his name, Earl was taken to his room.

Children's Village was an entirely unfamiliar environment for the teenager. Yes, it wasn't his first group home, but he had learned to survive on the streets. There were no rules when he was on the streets; it was his turf, and he could do whatever he wanted. But now, he had a bedtime, lunchtime, waking up time, and no dogs. Earl had to learn how to survive the institution all over again, and at that time, he couldn't even change his clothes.

As time went on in Children's Village, he began to settle in. His "Crazy Earl side" started to show up, and he found ways to live by his own rules as much as he could.

Young DMX discovered his love for running while in Children's Village. He joined the track team, and, as seemed to be the case with everything else that he did, Earl was the top performer.

But the track team wasn't the only good thing that happened to Earl while he was in Children's Village. In the group home, he would fall in love with something that ended up being much more important to him; Hip-hop.

The cottages in Children's Village School for Boys were arranged geographically. This meant that kids who came from the same parts of the country would most likely end up being assigned to the same cottage. This ended up being a stroke of good fortune for young DMX because everyone from his cottage was from Westchester County and New York. And one thing all of them had in common was their love for hip-hop which at that time was a new genre of music.

BECOMING DMX

Hip-hop was just coming onto the music scene at the time. The music was considered "ghetto," and so it wasn't played often by radio stations. R&B and Rock music were dominating the airwaves then. So, the kids in Earl's cottage would put on the radio and spit rhymes over other people's songs that they heard – even if it wasn't a hip-hop song.

At the time, DMX wasn't DMX... he was just Earl. And Earl had never come up with a single rhyme his entire life. So, while others were rhyming to the beats of songs on the radio and challenging themselves to see who could say the best rhymes, all Earl would do was stand to the side and enjoy the music.

Earl soon got sick and tired of feeling left out, so when he was able to go back home to Yonkers to visit, he would record different episodes of Mr. Magic's Rap Attack show on the radio and memorize Whodini verses.

When he got back to Children's Village, he would say the Whodini rhymes and make the kids believe they were his. It worked. The others believed the rhymes were his and gave him the praise for such hot rhymes.

Hip-hop was quickly becoming a culture that all the kids were into. Some kids were breakdancing, some were rhyming, some were DJs, and those that couldn't do any of that were b-boys whose job was to stand around and look cool.

Looking to find his niche so he could fit into the hip-hop trend, Earl decided to try out beatboxing. It took some practice, but when he got the hang of it, beatboxing became his thing. He would look for mini beatboxing challenges on the street and show off his

talent.

Around this time, he met someone who would act as his

introduction to an actual career in hip-hop. His name was Ready Ron.

Ready Ron was a rapper from Brooklyn, and even though he

was more than ten years older than Earl, he liked the aggressive

attitude that DMX had when they met. Ron would ask Earl to

beatbox for him while he rapped. It wasn't long before Ready Ron

invited Earl to be his partner.

Ready Ron was a local celebrity of sorts in the hip-hop world.

When he wanted to do small shoes or performances, Earl's job was

to roll with him and beatbox. Earl agreed without even thinking

twice.

As Ron's partner, DMX needed a stage name. Not only was it the normal thing to do as a hip-hop performer at that time, but Earl also never really liked his first name. He had always felt it sounded very corny.

The Oberheim DMX drum machine was one of the best drum machines, and quite a lot of people were using it at the time. Earl was good with beats. Naming himself after the best beat-making machines wasn't a bad plan.

So, he chose the name DMX.

When he returned to school, Earl was no longer just Earl, nor was he Crazy Earl. He was now DMX. DMX, the Beat Box Enforcer.

But it would be a while before he became the DMX that the world knew. In the meantime, he was just a high school kid.

It was almost the end of the year 1985 when Earl was released from Children Village School for Boys. He was done with that institution: next stop, Yonkers High School.

Earl was just a freshman, but he was determined to run the place. He had a reputation; after all, not everyone could boast of having attended two group homes.

But he would soon decide that school just wasn't for him. However, that didn't mean he stopped going. Young DMX still had two reasons to keep going to school. The first was the track team. Earl ran almost every kind of race that there was as part of the track team, and he was the second-best on the team.

He was going to school, but that didn't mean he was attending any classes. At first, it was just lateness, but eventually, those turned to full-out absenteeism. Luckily for Earl, his coach really couldn't have cared less. He was still allowed to participate on the team and compete during meets.

So, the one time that anyone could be sure Earl would show up in school was during meets when he would turn up with his running shoes in his hand and not much else.

But there was one problem; even though Earl was a star on the track team, he was still a broke kid. No one was going to help him with money. No one could – not his mother or even his grandmother. Earl had to fend for himself.

And that was the second reason Earl kept going to school. He needed a way to get his hands on some money, and in his mind, the best way for him to do that was a robbery.

Earl's decision to get into robbery was born out of desperation, and well, laziness. Hustling took too long for him, but as a robber, all he needed was a few minutes, and he could get his hands on what his targets had worked for.

On Earl's first robbery job, he hit the jackpot. His victim was a lady walking out of the very same supermarket where he had gotten caught while trying to steal pies when he was just seven years old.

He hid in the bushes for hours, waiting for anyone that seemed like the perfect target. When he saw the lady pass by, he jumped out of the bushes, stole her purse, and ran. That day, he scored more than one thousand dollars from that single operation. Needless to say, Earl was hooked.

Robbery became his single obsession. School work wasn't nearly as important. H showed up at school frequently, but only because Yonkers High School was a great place to rob people.

His only weapon was Blacky, the huge dog he had stolen from the junkyard. Blacky wasn't just a weapon; he was an accomplice. When he wasn't being set on Earl's victims, Blacky was snatching bags from their hands for his owner.

Robbery gave Earl a thrill. He began to do it as a full-time job. It was his hustle. Young DMX began to do his hits on a schedule. He would rob three times a day; before school, after school, and late at night.

Before school, his victims were mostly people going to work or school. All he had to do was walk like one of them, push up on them, and take whatever he had his eyes on or whatever he could get his hands on. His victims didn't even need to know that they had

been robbed.

The afternoons and evenings were a different case. Most

times, Earl would rob them right to their faces. And that was his best

way to rob; face-to-face. Earl was never a fan of breaking into

people's homes because, in those cases, he never knew what he was

getting into. When robbing people in person, he was in his comfort

zone.

He became so good at robbing that he didn't have to wait for

hours like he had to do during his first robbery operation. He knew

the best times, the best locations, and the best victims to target. At a

point, he even had a little robbery crew of sorts with two of his

friends.

Things were going okay for Earl. He was doing alright with the cash he got from his victims and from selling whatever items he stole. Things weren't exactly comfortable yet, but they were better than when he had zero.

Then things started to go south. First, Blacky died. Killed by two shots from the gun of a cop. To add to that, he had a drug problem. And it was Ready Ron's fault.

A few years before Blacky died, Ron had introduced Earl to what he described as "the new thing on the block." It was a *woolie* – a blunt that was laced with crack cocaine. But Earl had no idea.

Before that, Earl wasn't new to taking drugs. He drank, and smoked weed, and even did some street drugs like mescaline. But these didn't have much of an impact on him. He would take them and forget about them until he came across another blunt or another bottle or until he felt like messing with some drugs. They had no lingering effects, no addictions. But with the woolie, it was different.

Thinking the woolie was just another one of those drugs and wanting to experience the high that Ready Ron promised it would give him, Earl smoked the drug.

Eventually, Earl would find out what was really in the woolie. He would discover that, contrary to what he thought, it wasn't just another one of those drugs. It contained one of the most addictive drugs on the street. But by that time, it would be too late. Earl had gotten into something he couldn't get out of as easily as he had jumped in. He would battle with the cocaine addiction for the rest of his life. Though decades later, after DMX's death, Ready Ron would deny ever being the one to introduce him to crack.

Earl's robbery took another turn. He was no longer just doing it to afford food to eat or to have some spending money for clothes and other things. He didn't even have the luxury of doing it for the thrill as he used to before. Now, he had an addiction to feed and voices in his head to silence. Earl was robbing to survive before, but now it was different.

It got so bad that on one occasion, young DMX went to school with a sawed-off shotgun taped to his leg. At that point, he didn't care about anyone or anything but the fact that he had to have money to feed his addiction.

Even after such a drastic move, Earl ended up with nothing more than a couple of dollars. But that move cost him a whole lot. Just a few days later, Earl ended up being sent to jail.

Industry Institution, a facility for juvenile offenders located just outside of Rochester, was the jail that Earl was sent to. It was a minimum-security facility with no gates, fences, or barbed wire surrounding it. The Industry was located in an isolated environment. There was no town around it for many miles, and it had very few guards making sure the children in the facility kept put.

Earl's sentence was two years long, but it didn't take him too long after being checked into the facility that he made up his mind that he was not going to stay that long.

So, he and one of his cellmates, who was almost as wild as Earl was, started to plan their prison break. It was December, the weather was cold, and there were no cities or towns anywhere in sight. But that didn't stop the two boys. They were determined to make it out of there, and it seemed like they'd rather die trying to escape than stay penned up for much longer.

They took a few days to plan and prepare for their escape, hoarding clothes to keep warm while outside. Once they were ready, they went for it.

All they needed to get outside the facility was to knock down one guard, and they were good to go. Or at least they thought they were, then the dogs started running after them. The guard must have somehow triggered an alarm. But even guard dogs weren't going to cause DMX and his determined cellmate to give up. The woods outside were dark, and dogs were on their tail; the two boys couldn't even see the dogs they were being chased by. Yet, they thought they could outrun the dogs, so that's exactly what they tried to do.

And they succeeded, almost. After a few minutes of running, one of the dogs latched on to the back of Earl's leg, bit him, and refused to let go. Somehow, Earl was able to get the dog off him.

With an injured leg that was bleeding badly, Earl continued his

journey.

Almost miraculously, the two boys had managed to escape

the dogs. They headed to the home of Earl's cellmate, keeping away

from the highways to avoid the chance of getting stopped by a cop.

They walked for days through small towns and stretches of

farmland that may have seemed endless. The two boys got very little

sleep, no proper food, and no shelter against the cold December

weather.

Finally, they arrived at his cellmate's hometown, and they

both went to one of his friend's houses to stay in her basement. The

basement was large and spacious, but most importantly, it was

somewhere warm. Not too long after they got there, Earl's former

cellmate and fellow escapee left him, saying he was going to go home to get some money. Earl, of course, believed him. After all, he

didn't have a reason to think that his ally would lie to him. Both of

them had promised each other that they were in it together. But

after he left, he never came back. Earl was alone in that basement

until the next day.

The next day, the owners of the house came down into the

basement and found Earl hurdled up in a corner with blankets,

fighting against the cold. His former cellmate had called and told

them about his presence in their basement.

Fortunately for young DMX, the occupants of the house were

incredibly nice to him. They fed him, played games with him, took

care of him, and they even made him a cake for his birthday, which

had just passed. But more important to Earl than all of this was that

the owners of the house didn't call the cops on him. Even though

Earl never saw his former cellmate again, he had gotten a good setup

and was comfortable.

On the last day of Earl's stay at their house, the owners did one last thing for him; they gave him some money for a bus home. It was just before New Year, early in the morning, when Earl got back home. He looked a mess, clothes tattered, and the wound on his leg where the dog had bitten was infected.

Finally, at his mother's house, Earl wasn't expecting what he met; his mother gave him nothing more than a cold welcome. So, he left for the one place where he knew he'd be welcomed with at least a little bit of love – his grandmother's house.

Earl stayed a couple of days at his grandmother's place. He was officially an escapee. But that wasn't going to last for much longer. Just a few days after New Year's, there was a knock at his grandmother's door. It was the police. They had come to get him. Earl's mother had called them and led them there.

Earl was taken back to juvenile detention, but this time, it was different. Now that they had seen what Earl was capable of, they weren't going to make the same mistake they made the last time. Earl's new juvenile detention facility was named McCormick Juvenile Institution, and it was nothing like Industry.

Where Industry had almost no security, McCormick had gates, fences, and barbed wires on these fences. McCormick was also swarming with guards – guards that had guns.

Earl knew he had met his match at McCormick, and he never even thought of escaping. He knew he would never make it. Instead of plotting an escape, Earl used the time to think of other things, including his career as a beatboxer. The result of all this time thinking about his beatboxing career brought him to the decision that he wasn't going to be a beatboxer anymore.

Working with Ready Ron was good fun for Earl, but after nights spent beatboxing, Ready Ron was always center stage, getting all the attention and all the girls.

Earl decided he was done with beatboxing. He wasn't okay being the background kid who did nothing but gives a beat while the star of the show did his thing. He had made up his mind. Goodbye to DMX, the Beat Box Enforcer. Earl was going to be a rapper.

DMX THE RAPPER

Becoming a rapper wasn't too difficult for Earl. He had a lot of time on his hands, morning and night, to write rhymes. Plus, he had picked up a lot from Ready Ron and knew how to move the crowd.

With the boom box that he had brought from home providing him with background music, Earl wrote rhymes about everything he knew and the world around him. He soon found rapping to be an outlet for expressing his thoughts and freely talk about whatever he wanted to.

By the time he returned home from his stay in McCormick, Earl was no longer just Earl. He wasn't Crazy Earl, and he wasn't DMX the Beat Box Enforcer. He had become DMX the Great.

DMX's first performance was to a bunch of eight- and nine-

year-olds in the parking lot of the Nepperhan Community Center,

down the street from his grandmother's house. Inspired by the

movie Krush Groove, Earl had gone to the head counselor at the

community center and pleaded with her to let him do a show. After a

lot of pleading from himself and requests from other kids to let Earl

perform, the head counselor eventually gave in on the condition that

his rap didn't contain any bad words.

While the audience of his first performance wasn't the typical

rap crowd other rappers like Ready Ron would get, and his rhyme

featured mainly sesame street characters, it was good enough for

young DMX.

His performance was great; everyone enjoyed it, even the

community center's head counselor herself. However, despite all his

pleas, she wouldn't let him throw a full-out party with a DJ and

everything.

It would be a while before DMX could perform again. With no plans of ever going back to school and his mother finally letting him stay at his grandmother's house, Earl spent quite a lot of time writing rhymes. But between writing rhymes and hanging out at his grandma's house, doing next to nothing, Earl had a lot of time on his hands.

In typical Earl fashion, he picked up another vice – stealing cars. Car theft was not like the robberies Earl used to do on the streets. The robbery was a means of survival for him. He enjoyed the rush it gave him, but more than that, he needed to do it to get food to eat and clothes to wear. Stealing cars was purely for fun to Earl. He wouldn't sell them or their parts; he didn't even need them to go anywhere. Earl had found a new hobby, and he wasn't planning to give it up anytime soon. But soon, he would be forced to.

It happened one day when Earl and a friend he had made in Children's Village School for Boys took a joy ride through the

Hamptons. In an all-white, rich folks' neighborhood like that, the two young black people must have stood out like a sore thumb.

The police caught both Earl and his friend, but because his friend was a minor, he got off. Earl, on the other hand, was facing an entirely different situation. He wasn't a minor anymore, and to make things worse for him, he was already on probation. His punishment this time would be more serious than anything he had gotten before. Earl got sent to jail. But this wasn't juvenile detention, and it wasn't a group home. It was the real deal. Earl had officially become a convicted felon.

Earl got to spend his jail time at the Farm. It was the minimum-security branch of Suffolk County Correctional Facility in Long Island. The Farm wasn't so bad, especially not for Earl. The facility was mainly for inmates who had committed nonviolent crimes like drunk driving or theft. The living situation put them in groups in dorm-like spaces called mods, and the inmates had the freedom to read, play cards, talk to each other, etc.

Earl had spent enough time in juvenile detention centers. From the Youth Division of Valhalla, the prison in Westchester County, to Industry Institution, to McCormick Juvenile Institution, Earl wasn't new to the prison system. It wasn't too long before he – and two other guys he had ganged up with – started to run the place. Earl and his crew would intimidate their fellow inmates into getting them stuff like money, food, and even weed. They took advantage of whoever they could and ordered them to do whatever they wanted.

This worked out fine for the three men – Earl and his gang. Until one day when it all went south. One of the inmates the gang was using to their biddings set them up, and Earl and his two friends were charged with extortion.

Earl said goodbye to the minimum-security jail he was in and was transferred to the main unit of the Suffolk County Correctional Facility. His first week there was spent in "the hole" – a six-by-nine-foot space that he was never allowed to leave. It was dark, and there was hardly even any space to move around. To top it all off, his guards were cruel.

DMX had been moved from a relatively comfortable, minimum security jail straight into solitary confinement. Yet, it didn't bother him as much as it should have.

Maybe if he hadn't spent all that time in isolation away from all the other kids while he was in Andrus, the hole would have gotten into his head. Or maybe if his mother hadn't punished him by locking him up alone in his room for all those months on School Street. Maybe if he was someone else, the hole would have been a nightmare. But not DMX.

The hole should have driven him nuts – away from people in a dark, tiny room, surrounded by inhumane guards. It probably would have, but DMX had been through juvenile centers, survived life on the streets with no one but dogs as his companions, lived in group homes, and much more. To DMX, the time in solitary was an opportunity to think. Think and rhyme.

One week in solitary, and DMX had written more rhymes than he had ever before. It was a breakthrough moment for him. Rapping was no longer just a hobby or for fun. It was now a real thing.

After being released from solitary and allowed to join the regular population, DMX wasn't planning on letting his rap talent go to waste. He battled with almost everyone on his cell block who thought they could take him, and he beat them all. Everyone knew rhyme was his thing. But there was someone else out there, and word around the block was that this new guy could give DMX a run for his money. His name was K-Solo.

K-Solo was supposedly the cousin of Erick Sermon, who at that time was a big star in the hip-hop world as part of a duo called EPMD. Rumor had it that K-Solo was so good; he would have been big already if he wasn't stuck in jail.

Earl was itching to battle this guy and see what he was made of. One day, he finally got the chance to do just that. It was during their daily one-hour-long recreation time, which was the only time the inmates were allowed to go outdoors.

K-Solo was on the other half of the yard with the inmates who were in Protective Custody. The two halves were separated by a fence, but that didn't stop them. And for the entire hour of recreation, they battled each other from opposite sides of the fence.

The rumors about K-Solo weren't just empty hype. The guy was good, and his rhymes were hot. The two went back and forth for an hour. For every hot verse that DMX dropped, K-Solo seemed to have a response that was just as good.

In the final round, just before their recreational period was over, DMX managed to steal a win, dropping a rhyme that had a style unlike any that the others had ever heard. DMX had his first official win, and it was no small feat.

That battle did more than boost DMX's rep in the facility; it gave him a new buddy. Even though the two never battled again, mutual respect of sorts had formed between K-Solo and DMX, bonding the two men together. The two of them would sit and talk to each other through the fence during their recreation hour.

Next on DMX's agenda was to stay out of trouble so he could leave jail and get back to Yonkers as fast as possible. He had plans now that he'd proven to others and himself how good of a rapper he was. DMX's idea was to link up with someone who'd help him create tapes of his rhymes which he could sell on the streets.

Eventually, to DMX's relief, the time of his release came, and he went back home to Yonkers. Unfortunately, his plan to make a tape didn't become a reality because, in less than 24 hours of being out of jail, Earl was arrested and sent right back for getting into a fight.

Earl seemed to be in a cycle. Anytime he got released from jail, it would be just a few days, and then something would happen, and he would get arrested again. But this wasn't all bad because jail time allowed Earl to work on his rap, write new rhymes and maybe even improve his old ones.

THE HUSTLE

In 1988, Earl was finally out of jail long enough to set things into motion. He found a DJ, recorded his rhymes, and made copies of them to sell on the streets. Soon, DMX the Great was almost running the rap scene in Yonkers. He would challenge anyone he could to rap battles, bringing his A-game every time, showing no mercy.

Most of the time, Earl's opponents would leave the battle at a loss and embarrassed. They weren't just battles to DMX, they were wars, and he was out to win. Everything goes in war; Earl wasn't afraid of being too vicious or going too far. When he had finished everyone he could in a rap battle, and he was officially the winner, Earl would use the opportunity – and the buzz he had created by winning – to sell his tapes.

X's rhymes were fire. There was no question about it, but he needed more than killer songs. He needed killer beats to match.

Finding someone with the right equipment and skills to create the kind of music that DMX wanted proved to be a difficult task for the rapper.

Then he heard about Lord Kasun.

Lord Kasun was the complete package. He had the right equipment, the right records, and the skills to make magic. Lord Kasun's beats seemed to be the one thing that was missing from DMX's rhymes. Earl's songs were transformed, and he felt more like a rapper because he could finally create proper songs – complete with the hooks, verses, and all.

Earl was that much closer to becoming a full-fledged rap artist, and he knew it. But he wasn't planning on slowing down or becoming comfortable. DMX began to take his rap even more seriously. It became a science to him. He was driven to understand all the principles he could master of the art to consistently creating winning rhymes every time.

DMX's tapes were doing good on the streets, and soon, he'd have the chance to test if his music would do just as good at a live performance. The first club he performed at was named The Palace. It was an R&B club located in New Rochelle, New York, which had a talent show every other week. Earl signed up.

It was the day of the talent show, and Earl and his cousin, Mike, were in The Palace. While he waited for his turn, DMX observed his competition as they performed. He was confident that the majority of them had nothing on him. They would be easy to beat.

Even though Earl didn't have to bother much about his competition, he was still worried. His regular crowd was in Yonkers.

New Rochelle was new turf, and these were different people. They weren't Yonkers folks on the streets of the ghetto. They were New Rochelle people in a club.

By the time Earl got on stage, he had realized he had nothing to be nervous about. The crowd loved him, and his rhymes had them shouting and cheering him on for a full five minutes.

Needless to say, DMX won the talent show.

DMX's rep as a rapper was spreading quickly. At the time, the biggest rapper in Yonkers was a kid named Bill Blass. Bill MC-ed at parties and performed at clubs, and he was the talk of the town on the hip-hop scene.

Bill didn't have a record deal or anything, but in Yonkers, that didn't matter. He was a hero, and everyone knew who Bill Blass was.

Bill was the cousin of D Mac, a popular rapper that DMX had battled with and beat. Lord Kasun had recorded the battle and created a mix tape of it. Bill heard about this battle on the mix tape and challenged DMX to a head-to-head.

It was on. The date was set, and the location was fixed. Lord Kasun made the arrangements and performed the publicity – printing flyers and putting them up wherever he could to advertise the party to as many people as possible.

The hype that the party got was unlike anything Yonkers would see that year.

When the day of the rap battle finally came, the gymnasium was filled. People were everywhere, all looking for some space to watch the battle go down. There was almost no space for the performers.

DMX's rap was a full-blown verbal assault. By the time the battle was over, it was clear that DMX had won by a long shot. DMX, the nobody from the projects, had gone head-to-head with the biggest rapper in Yonkers – Bill Blass with the haircut, fancy clothes, and the ride – and had put him in his place.

Kasun made a tape of the battle, and soon enough, almost everyone in Yonkers was listening to the brutal beating DMX had given Bill Blass.

Everyone was pushing for a rematch between the two rappers. Bill Blass, probably looking to redeem his image, was up for it. This time, DMX planned and promoted the event by himself. He chose the Nepperhan Community Center as the venue and tried to convince the head counselor to let him throw the party there – just like he had tried to do a few years ago. This time, he was successful. The head counselor agreed.

On the day of the rematch, the venue was full once again. This time, it wasn't just Yonkers people. Folks had come even from Mount Vernon and New Rochelle. Word had spread about DMX, and everyone wanted to come and see for themselves.

Bill Blass had come to the battle ground prepared. He had created some new rhymes, ready to take on DMX. But it was clear that he was no match for the great X. His time as King of rap in Yonkers was over.

The night DMX had performed at the talent show at the Palace R&B club in New Rochelle, a guy named Jack MacNasty approached him just after his performance. Jack had a studio he rented, and he was looking for some rap talent. He wasn't promising Earl some superstar dream or anything. All he wanted to do was try and get a record deal for DMX and the other rap talents he worked with. DMX was down.

Earl and TQ, one of the rap talents Jack had recruited from the same talent show Earl had performed in, were taken to Jack's studio regularly. DMX wasn't a big fan of Shabazz, Jack's DJ, but on the bright side, he was getting to record in an actual studio, and he was creating good, professional-sounding material.

Jack compiled three of DMX's best songs on a tape. It was DMX's first actual demo. He sent this demo to record labels, trying to get DMX a deal with any of them.

Apart from record labels, one of the first places that Jack sent Earl's demo to was a hip-hop magazine called The Source.

The Source had a column they ran every month – "Unsigned Hype" – where they featured one new hip-hop artist who hadn't been signed to a record label. It would have been great to get an offer from any of the record companies Jack was trying to sell DMX's music to, but it would be even better to get featured in The Source's "Unsigned Hype" column. That way, getting attention from record labels would be a breeze.

Jack sent in a photograph of DMX as well as the demo. With that done, the pair couldn't do anything but hope for the best.

Jack MacNasty and DMX had worked together for a few months when Jack invited the rapper to move into his house so he could be closer to the studio, but also so Earl would stay out of trouble long enough for his career to kick off.

The deal sounded great. Earl would get a crib in New Rochelle, a neighborhood that was much nicer than Yonkers, and he didn't have to pay a dime in rent.

It was early 1990, and DMX and a few other artists that Jack was managing would perform at Jack's parties. One party, in particular, that was quite popular among the crowd was the one Jack threw on Thursday nights at a club called the Castle in the Bronx. It was called "Sneaker Thursdays," and everyone loved it because it was one of the few places people could go to listen to pure hip-hop – no R&B – without having to obey some dress code or other rules.

Jack would have famous hip-hop artists perform at the parties, and the House Party All-Stars, which was what he called the artists he managed, would open for the stars of the show. Of course, DMX didn't think much of the other House Party All-Stars. He didn't think much of the stars that they had to open for. He thought he could take them all.

One day, he got the chance to prove his point.

It was another Thursday battle, and a DJ battle had just

ended at the Castle. The crowd was already pumped up from the

thrill of the DJ Battle, but instead of starting up the music after the

battle ended, Jack decided he wanted DMX and another House Party

All-Star named TQ to perform.

DMX knew it was a bad idea, and to prove him right, as soon

as TQ got on stage for his performance, the crowd booed him. After

just one song, TQ's performance had ended, and it was DMX's turn

to go on stage.

Knowing the same thing that happened to TQ would happen

to him if he didn't do something about it, DMX had to quickly come

up with a plan. When he got on stage, he spotted a rapper whose rep

had spread throughout New York for his hot rhymes. His name was

Lord Finesse, and he was with his partner, Andre, the Giant.

DMX had found his plan. He was going to attack the two men, completely unprovoked. DMX threw his rhymes straight at the two men like it was a rap battle on the street. Once the crowd noticed what DMX was doing, they went wild. The two men he was dissing were getting mad, and they didn't have a way to respond. Then the DJ gave them what they were looking for. He stopped the music and asked the two men to come up so it could be a full-out rap battle, just like on the streets.

It was officially on. The attention of everyone in the club was on what was happening on the stage. Andre the Giant lived somewhere around the corner, and he was a local celebrity. His people were in the club, and everyone wanted to know who it was that had the guts to take on their man.

Jack MacNasty was against battling, especially when it was in a club like the Castle, during a party, and not on the streets. At that moment, with everyone's eyes on him, DMX was starting to have second thoughts as well. This wasn't Yonkers. It wasn't even New Rochelle. It was the Bronx where no one knew him. No one had bought any of his mixtapes or even heard about the legendary beat downs he had given Bill Blass on two different occasions.

He had started a battle between himself and two high-rep rappers on their turf. If he lost the battle in a place like the Castle while there were so many artists and people from record labels around, not only would he not be able to ever perform in the Bronx again, but his rep would also be destroyed. And his rep was the only thing he had as a rapper. That could be the end of his career which hadn't even started.

But DMX had already begun the battle, and he was going to finish what he started.

Lord Finesse and Andre the Giant got on stage, ready to face DMX. By this time, almost everyone in the club had rushed to the front of the stage to get a good view of the action.

The battle had begun. From his numerous rap battles on the streets, DMX had experience with taking on two people at a time, so he wasn't worried that his opponents outnumbered him.

At the end of the battle, DMX emerged as the winner. Things changed after that night for Sneaker Thursdays and the Castle as a whole. The party became more and more popular, and DMX's rep spread.

Not too long after, he was performing in Manhattan. It was during an annual talent conference called the New Music Seminar. This talent show was held in a large school playground called Rocksteady Park and was one of the most influential events in hip-hop at the time. Major record labels supported the show, and hip-hop enthusiasts from different parts of the country would come to watch.

DMX was one of the talents, and as usual, he was out to win. And that's exactly what he did. At the end of the talent show, he emerged as the winner of the Best Rapper award.

That was good enough to be the highlight of his day. He was going to take the award and show it off to the guys at Yonkers. It was like he had officially taken over the rap scene in NYC. But he got even better news after the show; The Source Magazine had called back, and they wanted to interview DMX for the Unsigned Hype column. It had been months since Jack had sent them the demo and a picture of DMX, and since they hadn't heard anything back, DMX assumed the worst – the magazine simply wasn't interested.

The recognition that DMX could get from being featured in The Source magazine as the best-unsigned rapper in the country was career-transforming. He wouldn't just be any ordinary street rapper. This was the chance for DMX the Great to become a household name.

One of DMX's next performances would be the biggest he had ever done at the time. It was at an event at Commerce High School, which would be headlined by some pretty big hip-hop stars in the country. It was a real concert, not a Sneakers Thursday at the Castle or any other night at a club. DMX's performance was supposed to be the first in the show, but he and Lord Kasun had left to find a spot to smoke weed. By the time they showed up at the concert, all the hip-hop performances but one had taken place, and the last group was setting up their equipment to begin their show.

DMX wasn't bothered. He was in Yonkers, after all, and that was his turf. He got on stage after the last performance was done.

With his five dancers behind him and Lord Kasun giving him fire

beats, DMX gave a performance that drove the crowd crazy.

The energy levels were through the roof during the concert,

and by the time it had ended, DMX was drenched in sweat. People

rushed him and Lord Kasun, asking for autographs and taking

pictures with them. DMX had gotten a taste of the life he had his

eyes on.

But unfortunately, it was just a taste and nothing more.

A lot of Earl's time was still spent looking for people to rob

and robbing them. He would walk the streets of Yonkers with

Boomer, his pit bulldog who was smart and well-trained, yet one of

the most dangerous dogs around.

Earl trained Boomer to act almost like he was a human being on the streets of Yonkers. What happened to Blacky, his dog that had gotten shot by the police, could never happen to Boomer. So, he trained him to fight, jump, and even go over fences.

One day while Earl was hanging out with and training Boomer, Jack suggested to Earl that they needed to sign an agreement. Jack was officially going to become his manager, and DMX didn't mind. He trusted Jack like he was an elder brother. DMX didn't think twice before signing the paperwork. What he missed was that instead of making him money from his art as he had always wanted, the management deal was going to keep DMX broke for a while and even get him into debt.

See, legally, Jack didn't have to pay for anything because he was the manager. X, on the other hand, was the artist. This meant he had to cover the costs of studio time, engineering fees, and other bills he simply couldn't afford. Money was seeping out, and it didn't look like there was any money coming in anytime soon. Jack wasn't

able to get any record label to accept DMX's demo. They always had

one complaint or the other. to some, DMX's voice sounded "too

rough," or he "didn't look marketable." Some didn't want to have

anything to do with him simply because he was from Yonkers.

Yonkers was a small town in New York that most of the bog shots at

the record label companies had never even heard of. To most of

them, X wasn't even from New York, and so he couldn't have had any

talent.

Unsigned Hype was supposed to be his big break, and

everyone seems to think that's what made DMX blow up. But that

wasn't the case at all. Even though he was the best-unsigned rap

artist, that didn't do so much for DMX. He had a truckload of talent,

hot rhymes, he knew how to move a crowd, and had won awards

and countless rap battles. But all this seemed to count for nothing.

He was still broke and struggling.

Unsigned Hype was a big achievement for DMX, no doubt. But it wasn't a big break.

Earl continued going back to the streets, robbing people to pay his bills and to survive. Not to mention that he still had an addiction that he was struggling with. DMX knew how to hide his struggle. He always gained the weight back, and most of the people around him didn't have a clue as to what was happening in his life. Sometimes, he would stay away for a few days after an episode until he was back to looking normal before heading back once more. DMX refused to let anyone in on his struggle, not even his girl Tashera who he was in a serious relationship with.

Earl would steal and sell anything he thought was valuable, gold chains especially. Once, at a party, he stole some guy's gold chain from his neck. The owner of the gold chain knew DMX had robbed him but didn't say a word about it. DMX thought he had gotten away with it, robbing a weak dude. But when he left the party, a group of about five guys was waiting for him. A fight started, and by the time it ended, Earl had given some of the guys a good beating, but he also ended up in jail. Six police cars had pulled up to the house where the party was happening and arrested Earl, three of his uncles, and his aunt Rhonda.

Being in jail wasn't so much of a bother for Earl anymore. He had been in so many times that he was beginning to get used to it. More than that, he may have even started to like it. Jail started to feel like home for the rapper. The hard, uncomfortable surfaces he had to sleep on didn't bug him too much, and neither did the bad food he had to eat. This time, he was to do his bid in Valhalla prison, Westchester County.

Earl would use his time in jail to think, create rhymes, and of course, battle. His rap battles became well-known among the inmates, such that most of them would look forward to the next guy who'd challenge X to a showdown.

At that time, his most popular rap in the jail and even on the outside was "Spellbound." The rap featured a style that was all DMX's creation. He would spell out almost all the words in the rhyme while maintaining the rhythm and sticking to the beat. It was the very same style he'd used to beat K-Solo, the rapper in Suffolk County Correctional Facility, who had proved to be the toughest rival he had ever faced during a rap battle.

Spellbound was his signature. It was the last song he performed during shows at clubs and was the final death blow in most of his battles.

Then one day, DMX's signature style was on the radio. One of his fellow inmates had heard it and told him, excited. DMX couldn't believe it. Then a few more people told him the same thing; they had heard his rap on the radio. DMX started to get more hopeful. Maybe his manager had somehow managed to pull it off. Then he heard the song himself and saw the video. It wasn't his rap. Someone had stolen his style and put it on the radio, and that person was K-Solo.

Earl had been betrayed by the one guy he had made friends with while locked up in Suffolk County Correctional Facility. The pair had hung out together, talked together. Earl had even explained to him how to do the style. Now K-Solo had taken the spelling style, made a rap with it, and his rap was quickly blowing up, getting played on national radio and getting all the attention that rightfully belonged to Earl.

It didn't matter that people all over New York knew the style was his. A star was being born out of DMX's talent, and that star wasn't him. The worst part? There was nothing DMX could do about it. He had to watch it play out.

For the next few days, X didn't do much but sit in his cell and make rhymes dissing K-Solo. It was at that moment that he created the song "Born Loser" about how he felt.

Despite it all, DMX still had fans in jail who wanted to hear him rap and take on others who thought they had lyrics.

But as it turned out, it wasn't just the inmates who were interested in listening to Earl rap. One of the corrections officers from his cell block was too. He had been listening to Earl rhyme for months, battling people all over the cell blocks. Earl found out this corrections officer's interest in his art one night when the CO walked up to him and asked about his rap. It was an unusual conversation; Earl wasn't used to having casual conversations with the corrections officers. He wasn't used to having any kind of conversations with them at all unless it involved disrespect or discipline.

The CO and his partner made beats and were interested in what DMX had to offer. X told him to talk to his manager, and a couple of weeks later, Jack came to visit him.

The corrections officer and his partner were looking to enter into the hip-hop industry as producers and were looking for some rap talent. DMX was down to work with them, but he had his conditions. They wanted a rapper; he could do that for them. But he also wanted something in exchange; he wanted to be free.

It was a deal. They paid his bond, which was worth $2500, and soon, he was out of jail. To keep his end of the deal, all DMX had to do was to go up to their place at Mount Vernon and rhyme to their tracks.

DMX went over to their place a few times and rhymed to their tracks, but he soon concluded that he wasn't interested in what they had to offer him anymore. Their tracks just weren't the kind of thing that Earl was after.

Apparently, the corrections officer and his partner weren't going to be Earl's ticket to the limelight. But another door that seemed like it had a lot of potentials to be legit would soon open up.

DMX was hanging out at his girlfriend Tashera's apartment in Yonkers when he met Joaquin "Waah" Dean. Or more accurately, Waah had met him. Waah had driven up to Tashera's place and called for DMX from the sidewalk. This was the second night that he had shown up at the place.

It was 3 a.m., and some strange guy, wearing a long trench coat and driving a car that Earl didn't recognize from around the 'hood, was at his door.

DMX answered the door with Boomer at his side, and a burner tucked in his sweatpants.

It turns out all the reinforcement may not have been necessary. Joaquin wasn't there to get him; he was there to talk business.

Joaquin was a hustler who was originally from Mount Vernon but called Harlem home. Waah's friend Heavy D had inspired him to give up drug dealing. When compared to the money that he could make in hip-hop, hustling on the streets wasn't worth it, and people were losing their lives. So, he decided he was going to enter into the hip-hop world. His new hustle would be hip-hop. It was clean, wasn't life-threatening, and it was lucrative. It didn't make much sense to Waah to continue hustling on the streets where every single day, he was risking getting sent to jail or worse.

Waah and his brothers wanted to launch their record label, but they were new to the game and didn't exactly know what they needed to make it happen. That was why they needed someone like DMX. He was talented, wasn't signed to a record label, but was familiar with the hip-hop landscape and was popular among hip-hop fans, at least to an extent.

When Waah gave DMX his pitch standing in front of his girlfriend's home in the middle of the night, DMX wasn't interested. It wasn't the first time he had heard that kind of talk. DMX was regularly approached by random producers and managers offering one kind of deal or the other. In the end, most of them were just talk and very little action. X wasn't going to waste his time on yet another one of this type.

He went back into the house.

But Waah wasn't like the rest; he was serious and ready to work. He was back again the next day, in the morning this time, knocking on one of the apartment's windows.

He had just one request this time that X would hang with him that day and see where he was coming from. DMX wanted to bring his dig Boomer along, and it was then that the two men discovered their mutual love for dogs. Waah had two pit bulls of his own. X liked Waah already. He jumped into his ride without a second thought.

X and Waah continued to roll together. Things changed for DMX after meeting Waah. Especially financially. Waah treated him well, making sure he had money in his pocket and quality weed to smoke.

It soon became clear that what DMX had with Jack MacNasty was coming to an end. DMX trusted Jack MacNasty like he would an older brother, but as he began to spend more time with Waah, he realized that Jack's era in his life was over. Waah wasn't a big fan of Jack because he thought the manager didn't have what it took to take DMX a step up in his career. And DMX started to agree with Waah.

Waah was so different from Jack. And it wasn't just the age gap between the two that was the issue.

Waah was all-action and could be ready for anything at a moment's notice. As soon as an idea was fully formed, he would make a move—no sleeping on anything. Jack, on the other hand, didn't seem like he was all in. He had a regular nine-to-five job, so hip-hop was more of a side hustle for him, and managing DMX was like a part-time job.

And it didn't hurt that Waah had the cash they needed to make the necessary moves. Money meant no more piling up of debts in studio fees. Money meant DMX and Waah could do whatever they felt was good for their careers whenever they wanted to. Choosing Waah was a no-brainer for DMX.

They needed a name for their game. Inspired by their entire life stories, the name Ruff Ryders came up, and as soon as they had the name, DMX and Waah drove down to Manhattan to get the record company officially licensed.

The first production agreement between Ruff Ryders, DMX, and Waah was for DMX to release an original single in six months. It didn't take much more than a week for Waah and DMX to decide on what two songs were going to be on the two sides of X's first twelve-inch vinyl single – "Born Loser" and "Catchin the Same Hell." What did take a while was scouting for the right producer with the rawest beats to complement DMX's rhymes. Their search came to an end when they found Chad Elliott, who was known as Dr. Seuss. Dr. Seuss

and Waah had met sometime back when he was working with

another group. The moment DMX heard his beats, he knew he had

found what they had been looking for.

By the time the songs were recorded and ready to be put on

vinyl, DMX's idea was to make about 500 copies and five them out

for free to key people in the hip-hop world like radio DJs and club

promoters. The aim was to get people talking about the songs and

get the attention of records stores. When that happened, they could

start selling copies of the single.

They made fliers to promote the single and distributed them

all through the projects. On the fliers, Jack also added the request

line numbers for local radio stations in the hopes that people who

knew and liked DMX would call in and request for his song to be

played.

It worked.

At least three radio stations in New York played "Born Loser." DMX's first official single to be released was doing well.

Just as Earl predicted, Jack soon started receiving calls from record stores all over New York, requesting copies of the single. They had to find a real distributor because Jack couldn't continue doing it all by himself.

Jack found exactly what they were looking for and more. He had found a company that was willing to manufacture and distribute "Born loser." But more than that, he had gotten a good chance at a record deal for DMX.

The name of the record label was Ruffhouse Records. It was a division of Columbia Records, which was one of the biggest music labels in the world at the time.

After meeting with Chris Schwarz, who was running Ruffhouse Records at the time, the record label struck a deal with X. It was for just one song, but a record label deal is a record label deal. Ruffhouse re-released "Born Loser" as a proper 12-inch single, but it never took off.

Some radio stations kept playing it, but outside of the New York area, Yonkers especially, the single didn't do so well. The label blamed the poor performance of the single on the song. But in the opinion of DMX and Waah, they hadn't put much effort into marketing the single. Ruffhouse hadn't succeeded – or even tried much – to create the hype that was necessary to sell records.

It seemed like DMX's career as a professional rap artist was over, and it hadn't even really started. Ruffhouse had practically relegated DMX to the backseat and turned their attention to some of their other talents.

Waah felt that DMX had so much talent that Columbia Records had no idea what to do with him. It was Waah's opinion that they could do much better on their own instead of relying on Ruffhouse Records the way they had done.

Waah, and his brother Darrin got a lawyer to officially cancel the management agreement between Jack MacNasty and DMX. They left Columbia Records as well. Ruff Ryders and DMX were officially on their own and were ready to take on the world of hip-hop.

Almost like a good omen to tell them they had made the right decision, Waah and DMX met someone who would prove to be very important in their journey. His name was Irving Lorenzo, and he was introduced to them by Dr. Seuss.

Irving was good. He had ideas, drive, and he was willing to put in some work. But there was one problem, he didn't have the equipment he needed to work his magic.

Waah believed in what Irving had to offer, so one day, he and DMX went to a music store and bought the equipment that Irving needed. Two thousand dollars in cash was what it cost Waah, but it turned out to be worth it. Together, DMX and Irving produced some great songs, including one called "Niggas Can't Touch Me Kid," which they decided to make his next single.

But this single ended up flopping as well, just like the first one had done. All of the effort that Earl and Waah put in to get popular

DJs and on-air personalities to listen to and help promote the single came to nothing.

For a while, DMX didn't have anything but two failed singles. He didn't have anyone either. Everyone on the streets of Yonkers seemed to be throwing him negative energy without even trying to hide it. Once, he had even narrowly escaped being murdered. The incident occurred at night at a basketball in the Ravine Project, Yonkers.

The basketball court was usually quiet at night, and Earl used it as a spot to chill with his dog Boomer and smoke some weed. The place was relatively safe because he could hear anyone who was coming towards his spot from the top of the path. So, sometimes he would even sleep there in the summers.

The night he almost got killed, he was standing in the area, having a conversation with a friend of his who had just picked his daughter up from the babysitter. They hadn't seen each other in a while, so the pair had a lot of catching up to do.

Suddenly, for some reason, DMX looked up. When he did, he saw three guys walking towards them with their hands in their pockets. He didn't recognize any of them, but one and something didn't seem right about him.

Immediately, Earl said goodbye to his friend and began to back away. In no time, he had broken into a full run. His tracks skills came in handy that day. The men pulled out guns and started shooting right at DMX. Earl ducked around the corner through a backyard fence and just kept running.

Earl's friend had hidden between two cars with his daughter when the shots began to burst out. It wasn't him they were after. It was DMX, and he had no idea why.

Soon, he found out.

Someone wanted him dead because one of Earl's robbery operations that he had embarked on that day had gone wrong. Earl had carried out the operation with a kid who gave Earl his gun for the robbery. That particular robbery ended up not being as lucrative as they had hoped. The victim had just forty dollars, and Earl needed much more than that. So, he chose to sell the gun. It was a black nine-millimeter piece that was bound to fetch a fair price.

The kid Earl had robbed with, as it turns out, wasn't the owner of the gun. And he had told the real owner that Earl had stolen it from him. and that was it. That was why he was shot at and almost killed that day. The owner of a gun he had sold wanted him dead.

It had been a while since Earl performed, but that was soon going to change. Waah had signed DMX up for a performance at a school called Drexel College in Philadelphia. It was the weekend of a big track tournament, and a lot of people were expected to show up, and DMX was to open for a music group called Das EFX.

Das EFX was a popular music group at the time, so quite a lot of people were expected to show up.

The energy from the crowd was nothing like what he was used to getting back home in New York. It wasn't one of his best shows.

Not long after, he did another stint in jail. This time, he was in solitary confinement for almost a year. Solitary confinement, as usual, was just another opportunity for Earl to be by himself and think. He was alone day after day, week after week, month after month. Sometimes, his uncle, Ray Copeland, who was his mother's youngest sibling and a social worker in Valhalla, would come to visit Earl. But that was the most company he got while in solitary. During that long year, Earl had a baby named Xavier with his girlfriend Tashera. Most of the time, he was alone with just his thoughts. That was when he wrote his first prayer.

DMX THE GREAT IS BORN

When he returned from his time in prison, Earl moved in with Tashera and their son at her apartment in the Mulford Gardens projects. Mulford Gardens wasn't the best place, but it was better and much less violent than the School Street projects where Earl had grown up and lived for most of his life.

Earl was happy with his girl and his boy, who he was so proud of. But unfortunately, there was one problem – Earl was still broke. So, he tried getting a job. Nothing he did seemed to work out, and soon, he was back on the streets trying to push his mixtapes.

That summer, he rolled with his younger brother Joe whom he had met up with while he was at Philadelphia for his performance. Joe smoked blunts with DMX and helped him sell mixtapes on the streets. That entire summer, DMX managed to not get into any trouble.

He would go to his grandmother's house and watch her beam with pride as he told her about his "Born Loser" single and told her about his songs and the performances he had done.

Earl would also take his son Xavier to her house. Grandma Hollaway was the one person that had loved and supported him unconditionally, and Earl was happy that he could make her proud of the things he had accomplished and of the father he had become.

However, things went bad quickly. Earl's grandma fell sick and was admitted into the hospital. She had cancer.

Every day, Earl went to the Yonkers General Hospital where his grandmother was staying, and he kept her company and took care of her for as long as he could until visiting time was over.

Then she died. It was September 21, 1994. Grandma Hollaway had died and left Earl for good. It was one of the most difficult things he experienced in his life.

DMX moved to Baltimore. It wasn't exactly something he had planned.

Money wasn't coming in from the hip-hop angle, and Waah and his brother Darrin decided to open up a hustling operation in Baltimore. DMX wasn't into hustling, but he went with them anyway. He felt like he needed to get out of Yonkers. At first, DMX joined them, working shifts at one of the two locations that Waah and Darrin had set up in Baltimore. But later on, he got fed up. Even though the operation was bringing in loads of cash, Earl just wasn't suited to that kind of thing.

After leaving the operation, DMX spent his time writing rhymes and walking the streets of Baltimore. DMX would take in the surroundings, study the community, and meeting random people on the streets. Some of the people he met on the streets turned out to be useful connections for him and his crew at Ruff Ryders.

X didn't rate most of the MCs at Baltimore. But one night, he almost lost a rap battle to one. His name was Nardo, and the night of their battle, the two rappers faced each other off for more than an hour. Nardo didn't seem to be running out of ammunition like the other rappers DMX had faced on the streets. That would probably have been his most difficult rap battle while he lived in Baltimore, but there was one that beat it.

And it went down in New York, not Baltimore.

Darrin, Waah's brother, had called DMX and told him to come down to New York. A new group of rappers called Harlem Knights had been welcomed aboard the Ruff Ryders ship. Harlem Knights were battling another group named Original Flavor in the Bronx, and DMX was backup in case they needed a little help.

X took the three-hour journey down to New York. Of course, DMX was not unfamiliar with Rap Battles, but this particular one was special and would be one of the most difficult rap battles DMX would ever have. It was between DMX and Jay-Z, the lead rapper of Original Flavor.

The battle between Original Flavor and Harlem Knights was heated. They had been going head-to-head for a while, but DMX and Jay-Z didn't get involved. But soon, it was obvious that the crowd wanted to see some action between the two top guys from both sides of the battle.

Jay-Z went first, and DMX tried to hit back the hardest he could. He wanted to stomp Jay-Z, and he wanted his win to be an indisputable one. But that would be more difficult than he could have hoped.

The battle was a close one. Jay-Z was good, no doubt about it.

Eventually, X moved back to Yonkers, and so did Waah and Darrin. The brothers created their recording studio because, really, what was a production company without a studio?

They called the spot Powerhouse, and it was the official home of Ruff Ryders.

There seemed to always be someone in Powerhouse every single night of the week. Producers would be testing out and creating new beats, and rappers would be spitting rhymes or sitting around

and writing new music.

There weren't any actual studios in Yonkers, and people

trying to get into the hip-hop scene were likely to be seen hanging

around the studio's lounge. But what this studio was known for was

all the rap battles it hosted. No other recording studio in

Westchester was as active as Powerhouse.

Rappers would come from far and near to test their skills.

There was always a beat playing, so the stage was always set for a

rap battle to go down.

Ruff Ryder MCs were known for putting all other rappers in

their place during rap battles. If the younger MCs didn't seem like

they were holding up pretty good against an opponent, they would bring in the big guns – DMX. Usually, once DMX got in the picture, it was over for the opposing team.

DMX's rep continued to spread, and he knew he was the best of the best. Everyone on the rap scene that had heard him drop his rhymes knew that he was hot. Yet, he didn't seem to be moving forward. He was still broke and living in the projects while everyone else, including Irving, who didn't have any equipment when they'd first met, seemed to be moving forward.

But that would soon change for DMX. His long-awaited big break was about to finally come. But first, something terrible would happen to him.

If there ever was a regular day on Ravine, that day was supposed to be one. DMX had done a lot of bad stuff on Ravine, but that day, it seemed like all his misdeeds would come back to bite him on the behind.

DMX had walked into a building and seen a gold chain on the floor. Immediately, thinking of nothing else but the money the chain could fetch him, DMX picked it up and put it in his pocket. Before he left the building, a bunch of guys confronted him about the chain, but as X's manner was, he brushed them off. Finders Keepers. After all, he hadn't even robbed anyone for the chain.

Before long, DMX had sold the chain. But on the streets, people kept telling him that they'd heard he had robbed a kid for his leather jacket and chain. DMX had no idea what they were talking about. The jacket he was wearing was one he had found earlier that day in someone's front yard. Plus, DMX didn't stick up kids.

None of it mattered. It wasn't long before the father of the kid who owned the chain and apparently, the coat X was wearing, found DMX. What happened after that was something X may never have expected. He was beaten up as he had never been before.

At first, the beatings came from just one person. Then, as if everyone X had ever robbed saw it as their chance to get back at him, more and more people joined in beating X.

They punched his chest, kicked his head, slammed against his back, and beat him every way they could. Earl had no strength left in him. he couldn't get up, he couldn't run, he definitely couldn't fight back.

Then he saw someone pick up a brick. It was one of his attackers, and if Earl had stayed there any longer, he could have been killed. Somehow, he summoned the strength to get up. At around the same time, the sound of sirens could be heard, and X

used the opportunity to get as far away as he could.

An ambulance found him lying in a pool of blood.

His injuries were bad. He had to have surgery to fix his broken

jaw, and he had to have his mouth wired shut. But while he was

suffering through the pain, good things were happening in the

background.

Irving, who now went by the name "Irv Gotti," had managed

to secure a meeting between X and Lyor Cohen, the president of Def

Jam Records. DMX's jaw was still wired shut, yet, even though he

could only eat liquid foods like smoothies and soups, X had somehow

managed to learn how to rap with his jaws wired shut.

The meeting date was set, and that night, Powerhouse was packed full. And right there in the studio among all the people was Lyor Cohen, the president of the biggest hip-hop label in the world at the time.

DMX stepped into the studio room, and everyone who was there before him stepped aside to let him do his thing. His jaw was broken, and he was in pain, but this was his chance. He was going to prove that no matter the pain, X was still X.

As usual, DMX got everyone who was listening to him captivated. His lyrics were real, and his emotions were even more real. There was something special about DMX, and Lyor Cohen saw it.

It didn't take any more convincing. Lyor was game to work with DMX. The rapper was thrilled. Not just because he had finally gotten the attention of a record label, but also because they weren't

trying to change him this time as most record labels had done in the

past. They were going to sell him to the hip-hop world just as he was.

X could do his thing and speak his truth, and no one was going to

interfere.

"Get at Me Dog" was the first single DMX released with Def

Jam, and seemingly overnight, the song blew up. The hottest radio

stations were playing it, and folks on the street were jamming to it. It

had become like an anthem.

People had finally found someone that could resonate with

them. Not million-dollar rappers in the fancy suits who rapped about

things they may never be able to relate with.

While the success of "Get at Me Dog" was unlike any of

DMX's other tracks, his professional career didn't seem like anything extraordinary to him. After all, some of his stuff had become popular

on the streets before. How was this time any different?

The answer came in the form of a huge check. Fifteen

thousand dollars was DMX's earnings from the single. All his doubts

disintegrated.

Soon, DMX was working on the songs for his first album and

getting movie offers.

The first movie he acted in was "Belly," where he played the

lead role.

In 1998, Def Jam released "It's Dark, and Hell Is Hot, " DMX's

debut album. The album blew up. It debuted at #1 on Billboard, and

in just its first week, it sold over a quarter of a million copies.

Lyor Cohen, trying to revive the record label from the deficit they had supposedly been running with and loving the response of people to DMX's rhymes, challenged Ruff Ryders. He wanted DMX to release another album that same calendar year. By December, it was done. It did better than the previous album, selling over 700,000 copies. Once again, it debuted at #1 on Billboard.

Two albums debuting at #1 within the same year; it was a record.

DMX was now a professional rap artist. He didn't have to rob anymore to survive. He not only had a wife that loved him and a son; now, he had the means to take care of them. It was more than 10 years coming, but it finally happened.

IT'S DARK AND HELL IS HOT

Earl Simmons struggled with drugs for most of his life. Since that moment that Ready Ron introduced him to crack cocaine, his life never remained the same.

DMX tried drug rehabilitation several times, but it didn't seem to work. Once, he had even canceled an entire string of upcoming performances just so he could focus on getting rehabilitated.

Drugs took over his life. And in the end, they may have ended up being the thing that would take his life.

It was approximately 11 pm on Friday the 2nd of April 2021. DMX had just had a heart attack and was in terrible condition. According to reports, this heart attack was a likely result of an overdose. The next day, it was confirmed to the public that Earl was on life support.

That night, as paramedics tried to resuscitate him, his condition seemed to get worse as his brain was deprived of oxygen for a while.

According to Nakia Walker, who was his former manager, Earl was in a "vegetative state." He had "lung and brain failure and no current brain activity."

DMX had fought his whole life. He fought people and even dogs to survive, fought with his addiction, fought during rap battles on the streets and in the clubs, fought to take his career to where it was. And at the age of 50, in that hospital bed, Earl had one more thing he had to fight.

But this was one battle he wasn't destined to win.

Even on life support, Earl didn't seem to be getting much better.

His 15 children and his entire family were together at his home and friends' homes around the same area. They were close to White Plains Hospital, which was where DMX had been admitted and was receiving treatment and medical care.

Whether or not he continued on life support or was taken off, it depended on his mother, Arnett. The choice was in her hands. And soon, she made the tough decision of asking that her son be taken off life support.

It was the 9th of April, 2021. DMX, at the age of 50 years old,

was taken off of life support. The record-breaking rap legend that

revolutionized the face of hip-hop had died.

DMX's music and life were inspirations. He was a man who

lived pursuing his dreams despite all the struggles that he went

through. Even after finally getting the money and fame he had

always wanted, X continued to stay true to himself and his people.

Final Surprise Bonus

Final words from the author...

Hope you've enjoyed this biography of DMX.

It was an utmost privilege performing deep research and bringing forth these information to the public for you to enjoy.

I always like to overdeliver, so I'd like to give you one final bonus.

Do me a favor, if you enjoyed this book, please leave a review on Amazon.

It'll help get the word out so more people can find out more about our beloved superstar to support his legacy! (Plus, it'll help me a lot too. Thanks in advance!)

If you do, as a way of way of saying "thank you", I'll send you one of my most cherished collection report– Free:

DMX: The Complete Discography Collection From The Beginning to the Very End

A complete list of all of DMX's work that was ever published (or not published). As a DMX fan, you'll find this utmost valuable and cannot be missed!

Here's how to claim your free report:

1. Leave a review right away.

2. Send a screenshot to: jjvancebooks@gmail.com

3. Receive your free report –"**The Complete Discography Collection From The Beginning to the Very End**"–*immediately*!

Enjoyed This Book? Then Check Out...

Get to know the "Real" Curtis "50 Cent" Jackson - Behind the Curtains

Here's Just a Taste What You're About to Read in This Concise 50 Cent Biography:

Things most people might not know about Curtis "50 cent" Jackson

Origin of the name "50 cent"

By 1996, after Curtis was signed by RUN D.M.C, he adopted the name 50 Cent, a name which was inspired by a petty criminal by the name of Kelvin Martin, who used the same name. When asked why he chose the name, he said he chose it because it was a metaphor for change, which implied that he was going to do things his own way that was drastically different from the way others did. In his words, "the name says everything he wanted to say because he had the same 'go-getter' attitude as the original 50 Cent."

The 9 Bullet story

Most people know that 50 Cent was shot nine times, but there are parts that most people don't know about the incident. For instance, during the shooting, 50 Cent said he had a gun while he was being shot at, and while he tried to fire back, he discovered that the gun was not cocked.

Also, another thing most people might know is that the doctors who were operating on 50 Cent tried to carry out a tracheotomy, a procedure which involved them opening 50 Cent's wide pipe and which could potentially destroy his chances of ever rapping again.

His grandma, however, refused. She said, "If he couldn't do his music, he would be lost."

Kanye West

50 Cent was not an entertainer and an avid businessman, but he was also someone who knew how to do PR and capitalize on controversies.

One of the incidents where he exhibited the knack for turning controversies to his advantage was when in 2007, while promoting his third album *'Curtis'*, he made an unprecedented move.
He announced publicly that if Kanye West sold more albums than his album (both albums were due to be released on the same date), he was going to quit music, and the fans bought into the challenge, thereby helping the both of them make good sales off their album.

When 50 Cent was asked in an interview about the results of the challenge and how he felt about Kanye emerging the winner, 'Kanye west gets the trophy, 50 gets the checks'.

Check it out here:

https://amzn.to/3eS9LOU

Or Scan the QR Code: